MW00534491

88 Piano Classics for Beginners

DAVID DUTKANICZ

DOVER PUBLICATIONS, INC.
Mineola, New York

Bibliographical Note

88 Piano Classics for Beginners is a new work, first published by Dover Publications, Inc., in 2011.

International Standard Book Number

ISBN-13: 978-0-486-48388-7
ISBN-10: 0-486-48388-6

Manufactured in the United States by Courier Corporation
48388602
www.doverpublications.com

Contents

Editor's Note

88 Piano Classics for Beginners is a collection of beloved musical themes specially arranged for the beginning pianist. Containing works from the core piano repertoire, this book also includes orchestral and chamber favorites—and more. These delightful works have been selected not only for their playability but also for the development of essential skills. Ears and hands can grow alongside one another with selections that focus on a particular skill: e.g., parallel thirds in Delibe's *Flower Duet,* chromatic passages in Fučík's *Entrance of the Gladiators,* and chorale playing in Tallis' *Third Mode Melody.* Fingerings have been provided as suggestions and should not be considered absolute. Each individual pair of hands will know what works best. Phrasing and pedaling have been left open in order to make the music less daunting. These should be penciled in as progress is made on each selection.

Glossary of Musical Terms

adagio, very slow

adagio cantabile, very slow and songful

adagio un poco mosso, very slow with a little momentum

allegretto, moving along, but not too fast

allegretto tranquillo, moving along, but not fast, in a tranquil manner

allegro con brio, lively, with a lot of vigor

allegro molto, very fast

allegro passionate, fast and impassioned

andante, walking tempo

andante cantabile, walking tempo, in a songful manner

andante grazioso, walking tempo, in a graceful manner

andantino, a bit faster than a walking tempo

a tempo, return to the original speed

cantabile, songful

cantado, singing out

coda, a concluding section

cresc(endo), getting louder

cresc(endo) poco a poco, getting louder, little by little

dim. E rit. (diminuendo e ritardando) poca a poca, gradually quieter and slower

D. C. al Fine (da capo al Fine), return to the beginning, then go to the "Fine" (end)

dolce, gently, sweetly

espressivo, espr., expressive

Fine, end

f *(forte)*, loud

ff *(fortissimo)*, very loud

fz *(forzando)*, strongly accented

ffz *(molto forzando)*, very strongly accented

grazioso, graceful

largo, very slow, solemn

legato, smooth, connected

leggiero, lightly

lento, very slow (a bit faster than *largo*)

lento espressivo, slow and expressive

lento placido, slow and placid

L.H., left hand

maestoso, majestic, stately

marc(ato), marked, accented

mf *(mezzo-forte)*, medium loud

moderato, at a moderate speed

moderato cantabile, songful, at a moderate speed

molto legato, very smooth and connected

molto marcato, very accented

molto rall(entando), held back a great deal

molto rit(ardando), slow down a great deal

molto staccato, very short and detached

mp *(mezzo-piano)*, medium soft

p *(piano)*, soft

pp *(pianissimo)*, very soft

ppp *(pianississimo)*, very very soft

poco a poco, little by little

poco cresc. E. rall(entando), slightly getting louder and held back

poco rall(entando), slightly held back

poco rit(ardando), slowing down a little

rall(entando), held back

rall(entando), poco a poco, held back little by little

rall(entando), E dim. poco a poco, held back and getting quieter little by little

R.H., right hand

ritardando, slowing down

sempre sostenuto, always sustained

sfz *(sforzando)*, strongly accented

sostenuto, sost., sustained

tempo di valse, a waltz

tranquillo, tranquil

vivace, very fast, lively

88 Piano Classics for Beginners

Carl Philip Emmanuel Bach

1714–1788

Solfegietto

Carl Philipp Emanuel was the son of the monumental Johann Sebastian Bach. He and his other brothers—Johann Christian, Wilhelm Friedemann, and Johann Christoph Friedrich—all inherited their father's wonderful talent and were musically famous in their own right. In this work, be mindful of the dialogue between the two hands, and use the "borrowed" fingerings (written above the left hand) to ease some passages.

Johann Sebastian Bach
1685–1750

Arioso in G

An *arioso* is a short piece, usually found in a cantata, where a story is sung by a solo singer. Keep the slow *Largo* tempo consistent, and try to shape the phrases as a singer would.

3
2
1
2
3
5
4
3
5
3
2
1
5
2

2
1
3
4
4
2
1
2
3
4
2
3
2
3
1
2
3
1
2
3
5

Johann Sebastian Bach
1685–1750

Affetuoso *from* Brandenburg Concerto No. 5

Bach composed six magnificent concertos for the Prince of Brandenburg. This melody is the opening of the second movement of the fifth. It is marked as *affetuoso,* meaning "affectionate."

Johann Sebastian Bach
1685–1750

Brandenburg Concerto No. 3 (opening)

This excerpt from the *Brandenburg Concertos* opens with a dialogue between the right and left hand. Keep the tempo steady so that the melody is uninterrupted. Also, use the left thumb on the repeated Ds to ease the right hand.

Johann Sebastian Bach
1685–1750

Menuet *from* Anna Magdalena's Notebook

This charming piece was found in a notebook of music Bach had written for his wife, Anna Magdalena. Some of the pieces were for teaching, but most were small gifts. Keep the mood merry and light.

mf

Johann Sebastian Bach

1685–1750

Invention in A Minor

Just like the other *Inventions*, this one was written to instruct new pupils. Here, Bach presents a challenging *arpeggio* workout. The music should flow evenly, helped by smoothness in the wrist and fingers.

Johann Sebastian Bach

1685–1750

Wachet Auf ("Sleepers Awake")

This wonderful melody is taken from a church, and translates into "Sleepers Awake." Keep a firm hold on the tempo – don't let the dips in melody slow you down. For the full effect, use dynamics to contrast different moods.

mp
f

p

Ludwig van Beethoven
(1770–1827)

Symphony No. 3 (theme)

Symphony No. 3 is nicknamed the "Eroica." It was written to honor "heroes" and was originally dedicated to Napoleon Bonaparte. Play the melody in a crisp manner, as if it were a military march.

Ludwig van Beethoven

(1770–1827)

Adagio Cantabile *from* Sonata No. 8

This famous piece is the opening to the second movement of the Piano Sonata No. 8, which is also known as the "Pathétique." The melody in the right hand should be played gently, while the left hand should be kept as even as possible. Be sure not to overshadow or overpower the melody

4
1
3
4
2
4
5
2
1
4
2
4
4
3
2
1
2
1
3
2
4
3
1
2
5

Ludwig van Beethoven
(1770–1827)

Romanza *from* Sonatina in G

This *romanza* is the second movement of the *Sonatina in G* found on the previous page. As with all *romanzas*, it should be played gently and tenderly, and not too fast. An *allegretto* is played slightly slower than *allegro*.

Ludwig van Beethoven
(1770–1827)

Piano Concerto No. 4, Mvt. II

Not only was Beethoven a composer, he was also a virtuoso pianist who premiered his own concertos. This particular concerto calls for extreme contrast, with the opening played loudly by the orchestra and then softly soothed by the piano.

Ludwig van Beethoven
(1770–1827)

Symphony No. 6 (opening)

Beethoven was very fond of the countryside, and it was in nature that he found most of his inspiration. Symphony No. 6 is a program piece depicting a day in the country. This opening movement is subtitled: *Awakening of joyous feelings upon arrival in the country.*

p
mf

Ludwig van Beethoven
(1770–1827)

Symphony No. 8 (opening)

The Eighth Symphony is considered to be one of Beethoven's lighter and happier works. It was first performed in 1814, and recalls the classical flavors of earlier music. The famous French composer Hector Berlioz said that this melody "fell straight from heaven."

Georges Bizet
1838–1875

Habanera *from* Carmen

The *habanera* is a popular 19th century Cuban dance introduced to Europe by Spanish sailors. Bizet composed this famous work from his opera *Carmen,* crafting the melody to its sly rhythms. This is a dance, so keep the mood playful and light.

12
1
15
3
1
17

Luigi Boccherini

1743–1805

Minuet *from* String Quintet in E Major

This popular work is the third movement from Boccherini's String Quintet in E Major. The ensemble consists of two violins, viola, and two cellos (often when depicted on screen, the second cellist is erroneously omitted). Note the syncopations and accent the upbeats at the beginning of tied rhythms.

Alexander Borodin
1833–1887

In the Steppes of Central Asia

Borodin was a chemist and gifted composer who was also one of Russia's "Mighty Five" alongside Rimsky-Korsakov, Moussorgsky, Cui, and Balakirev. This lyrical melody recalls the expanse of the Russian flatlands, known as "The Steppe." As an added Eastern flavor, the melody is played in a distant key before being echoed in the home key of C major.

Moderato

Alexander Borodin

1833–1887

Polovetsian Dance No. 1

This melody is from the opera *Prince Igor.* It was also adapted for the Broadway show *Kismet* and became popular as the song *Strangers in Paradise.* Play with a *legato* style and keep the melody flowing.

Johannes Brahms
1833–1897

Piano Quintet (opening)

This powerful melody begins a work for an ensemble known as a piano quintet: two violins, viola, cello and piano. To give it more strength, the melody is played by all instruments together. In the beginning, the left and right hands play the same notes, in octaves. Listen to how this helps project the sound.

Johannes Brahms
1833–1897

Hungarian Dance No. 1

This lively dance is the first in a popular set of 21. They're based on Hungarian and gypsy melodies that were in style at the time. Enjoy the upbeat and exotic character of the dance!

3
2
3
2
4
3
5
1
5
1
2
1
3
5
1
2
4
3
2
3
2
4
1
5
2
3
3
2
1
5
1

Johannes Brahms
1833–1897

Serenade *from* Four Songs

It's curious to note that Brahms never composed an opera. However, he did write over 200 songs! This sweet melody is set to a text by the poet Johann Wolfgang von Goethe (pronounced *Gér-ta*), whose poems were used by many composers.

Johannes Brahms

1833–1897

Symphony No. 4 (opening)

The fourth and last symphony was premiered in 1885 with Brahms himself conducting the orchestra. It quickly became an audience favorite and is still one of his most popular works. A key to practicing: there is a repeated pattern in the left-hand fingerings.

Allegro moderato

Johannes Brahms
1833–1897

Variations on a Theme by Haydn

Brahms was a fan of many composers and would write variations on their music, including Handel and Paganini. Here, he uses a Haydn theme known as *St. Anthony's Chorale*. The variation on the next page keeps the same bass, but decorates the melody by adding notes.

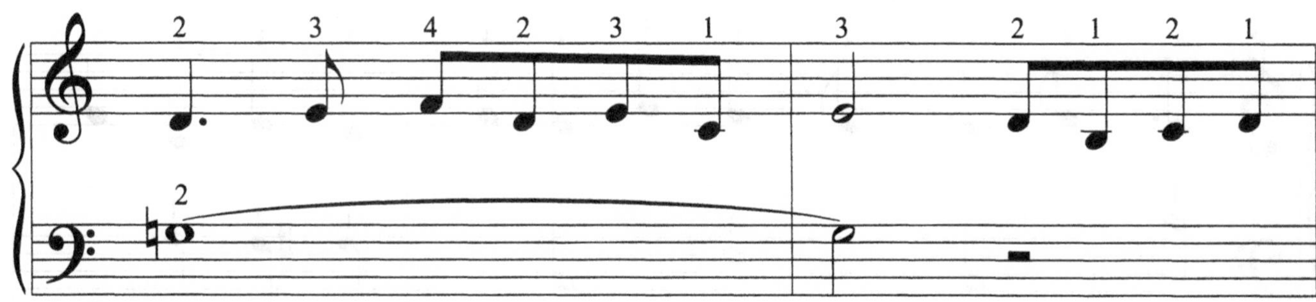

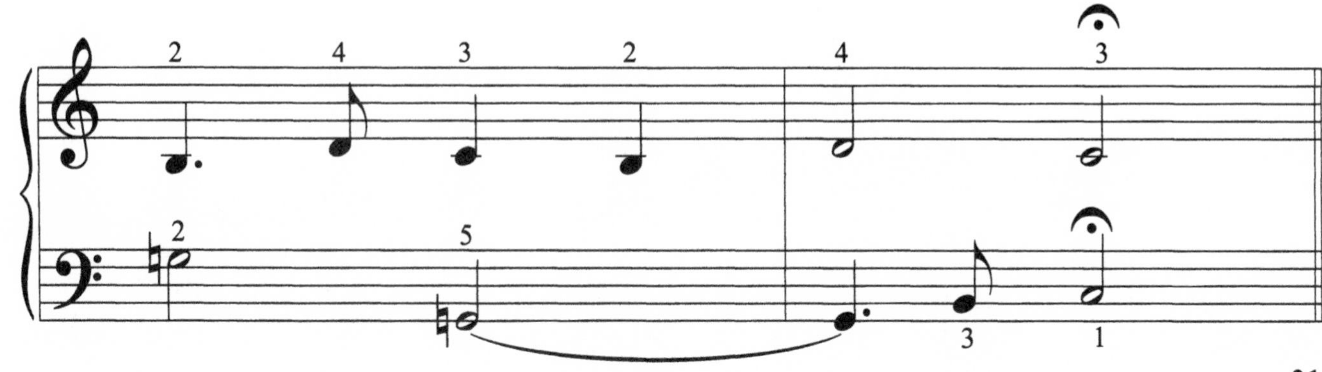

Max Bruch
1838–1920

Allegro *from* Violin Concerto No. 1

This brisk melody opens the third movement of Bruch's Violin Concerto No. 1. Bruch was a staunch supporter of folk music, and its influence can be felt in the rustic dance-like character of the work. Keep the notes crisp, and avoid playing with heavy fingers.

Frédéric Chopin

1810–1849

First Ballade

The lyrical slow theme from Ballade No. 1 in G minor, Op. 23, here in C major. Some say that this is the work that awakened the music world to the genius of young Frédéric Chopin. Listen to a recording of the original piece if you can: This perfect blend of heart-melting poetry and electrifying power has been called a "glowing masterpiece."

Flowing and songful

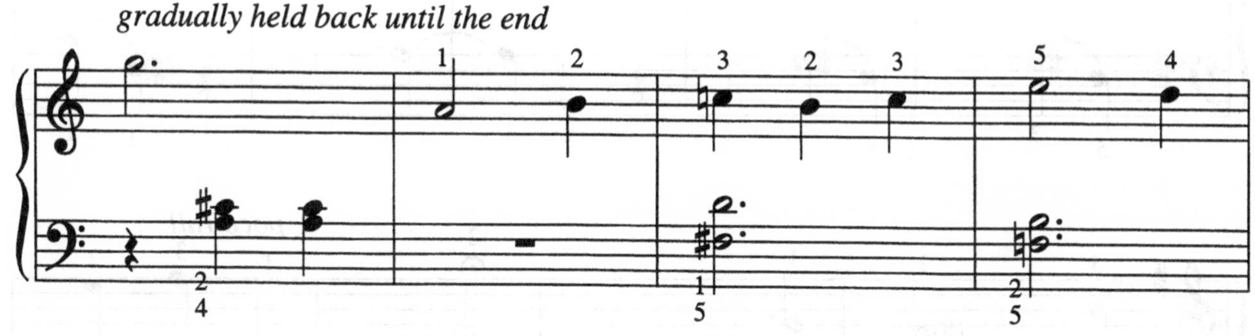
gradually held back until the end

(freely, slowly)

Frédéric Chopin

1810–1849

An Early Nocturne

The theme of the famous Nocturne in E-flat, Op. 9 no. 2 (here, in G major), composed when the frustrated and disappointed 20-year-old Chopin was still unknown to the music world. The title "nocturne"—meaning "night piece"—however, was invented by composer-pianist John Field, an Irishman almost 30 years older than Chopin. But it was Chopin who captured the world's attention with 21 magnificent nocturnes composed over the last dozen years of his life.

Slowly flowing

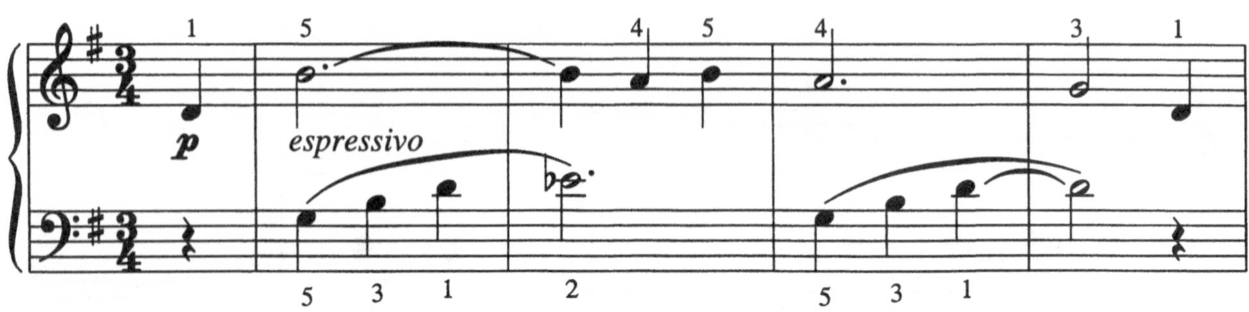

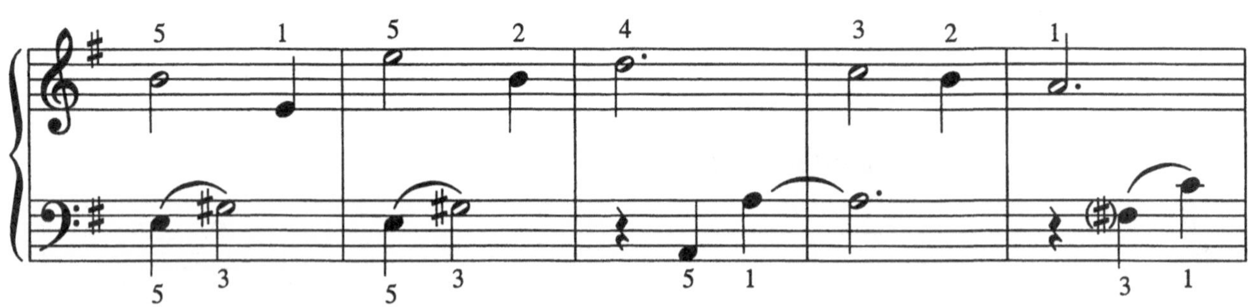

pp

mf poco accel.

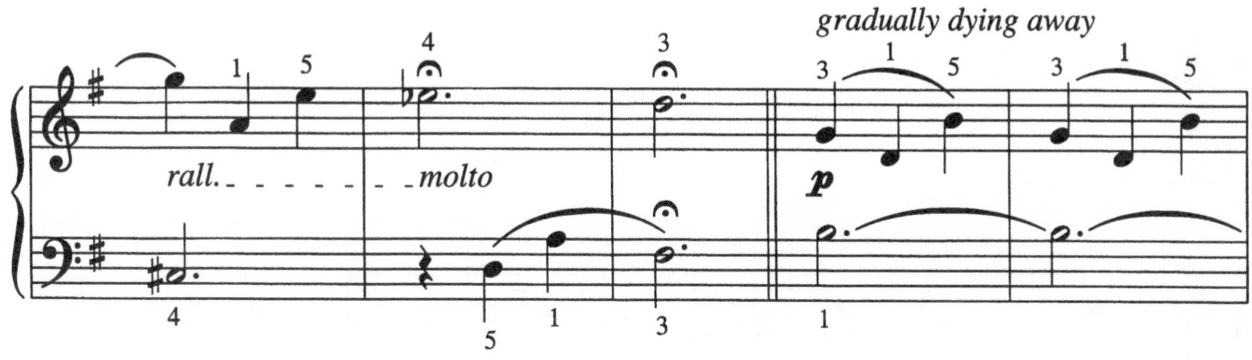
gradually dying away
rall. _ _ _ _ _ _ _ molto
p

Frédéric Chopin
1810–1849

Ballade in F

The main theme of the Ballade No. 2 in F major, Op. 38, still in its original key and rhythms. Composer Robert Schumann had dedicated one of *his* pieces to Chopin. So Frédéric returned the favor by dedicating this Ballade to *him.* Today, it seems unbelievable that great composers actually talked to each other, had dinner together, and played for each other! But it's true.

4
2
4
5
4
3
2
4
5
3
4
3
2
3
4
3
2

4
3
2
3
2
4
3
2
1
2
3
2
1
5
4
3
2
1

rall. poco a poco
1
3
1
3
1
2
3
4
1
2
3
4
1
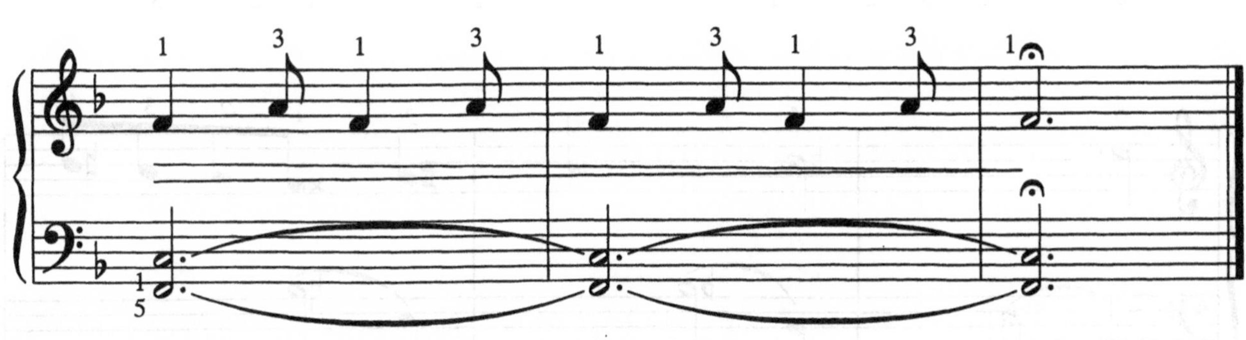
1
3
1
3
1
3
1
3
1
1
5

Frédéric Chopin
1810–1849

Grand Waltz in A Minor

The theme of the Grade Valse Brillante, Op. 34 no. 2. Close your eyes and imagine Paris, the most beautiful and fashionable city in all of Europe. Picture a candle-lit ballroom, music in the air, and elegant dancers in fine dress. Yet underneath it all is a hint of melancholy and sweet sadness. Was young Chopin thinking of his Polish homeland as he composed this quiet piece?

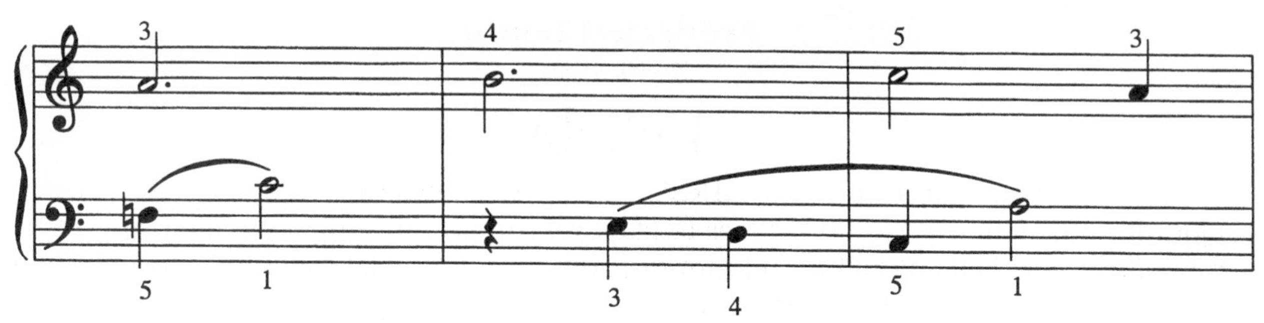
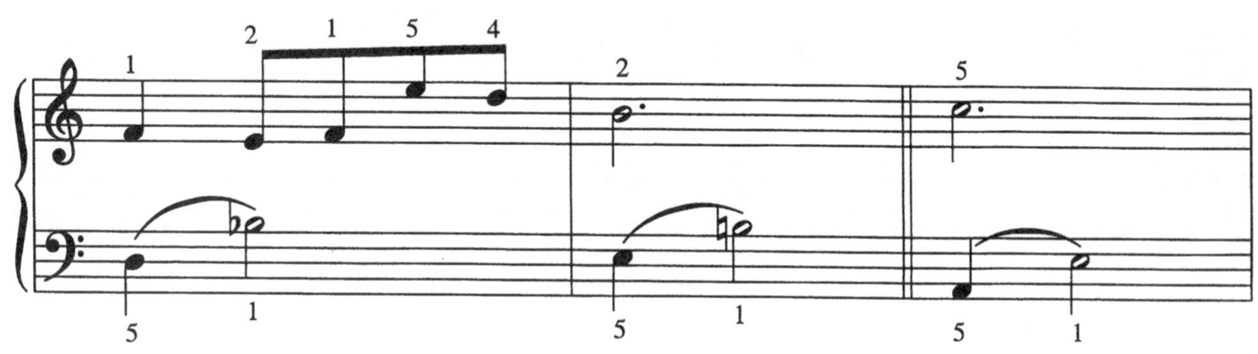

rall. - - - poco - - - a - - - poco
D.C. al Fine

Frédéric Chopin

1810–1849

Lullaby

The theme of Chopin's *Berceuse* [bear-SIRS], Op. 57, originally in D-flat major in 6/8. Here in G major, our notation in 3/4 is much easier to play, yet captures the original feeling. Since Chopin never married and had no children, it is not surprising that this lullaby is the only composition of this sort among his works. (Compare this to music by his contemporary Robert Schumann, who had a huge family and wrote many pieces for, and about, his children.)

Gently, with a quiet rocking motion

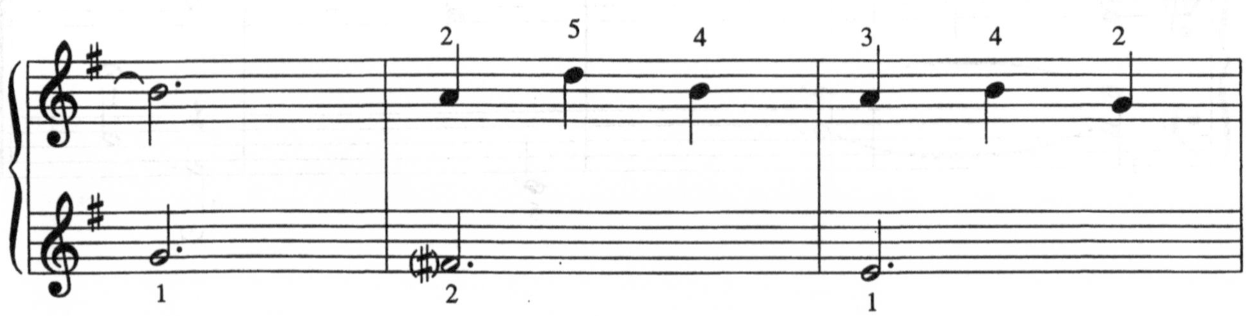

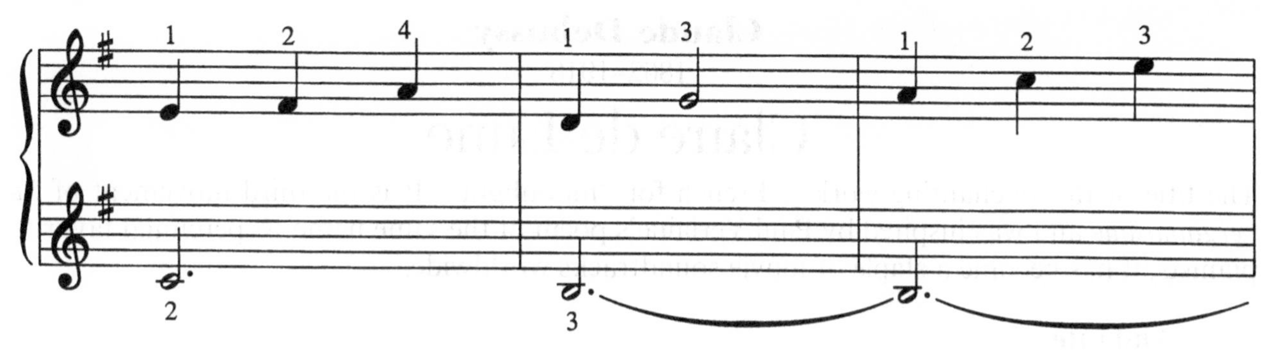

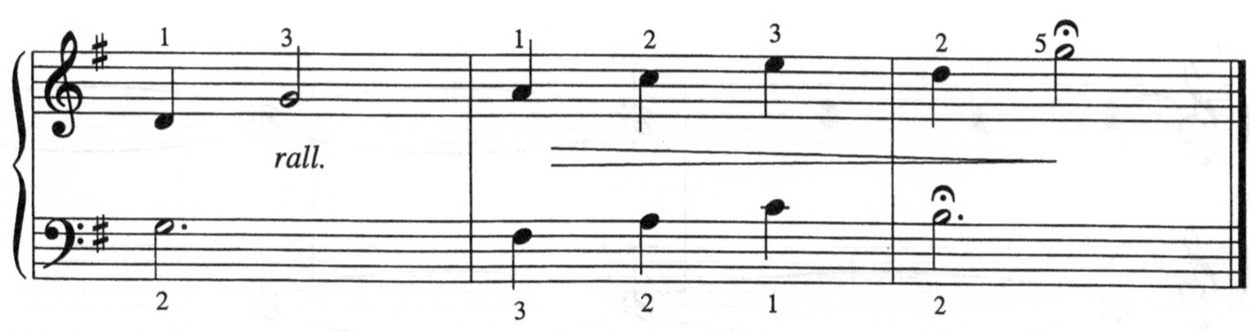
rall.

Claude Debussy

1862–1918

Claire de Lune

The title of this enchanting work is French for "moonlight." It is the third movement of *Suite bergamasque* and was inspired by Paul Verlaine's poem of the same name. A perennial favorite of pianists, it has become a staple of movie soundtracks worldwide.

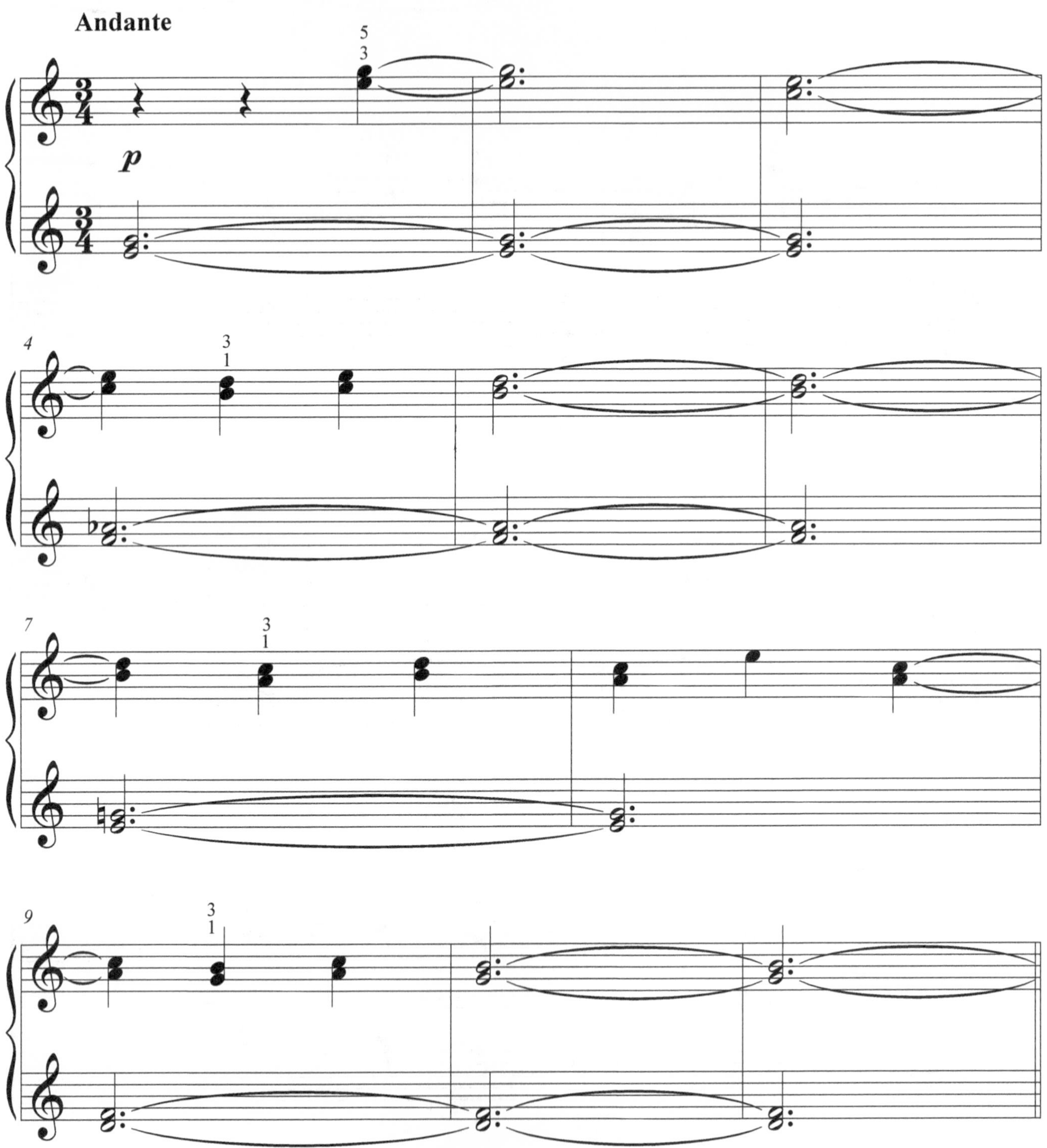

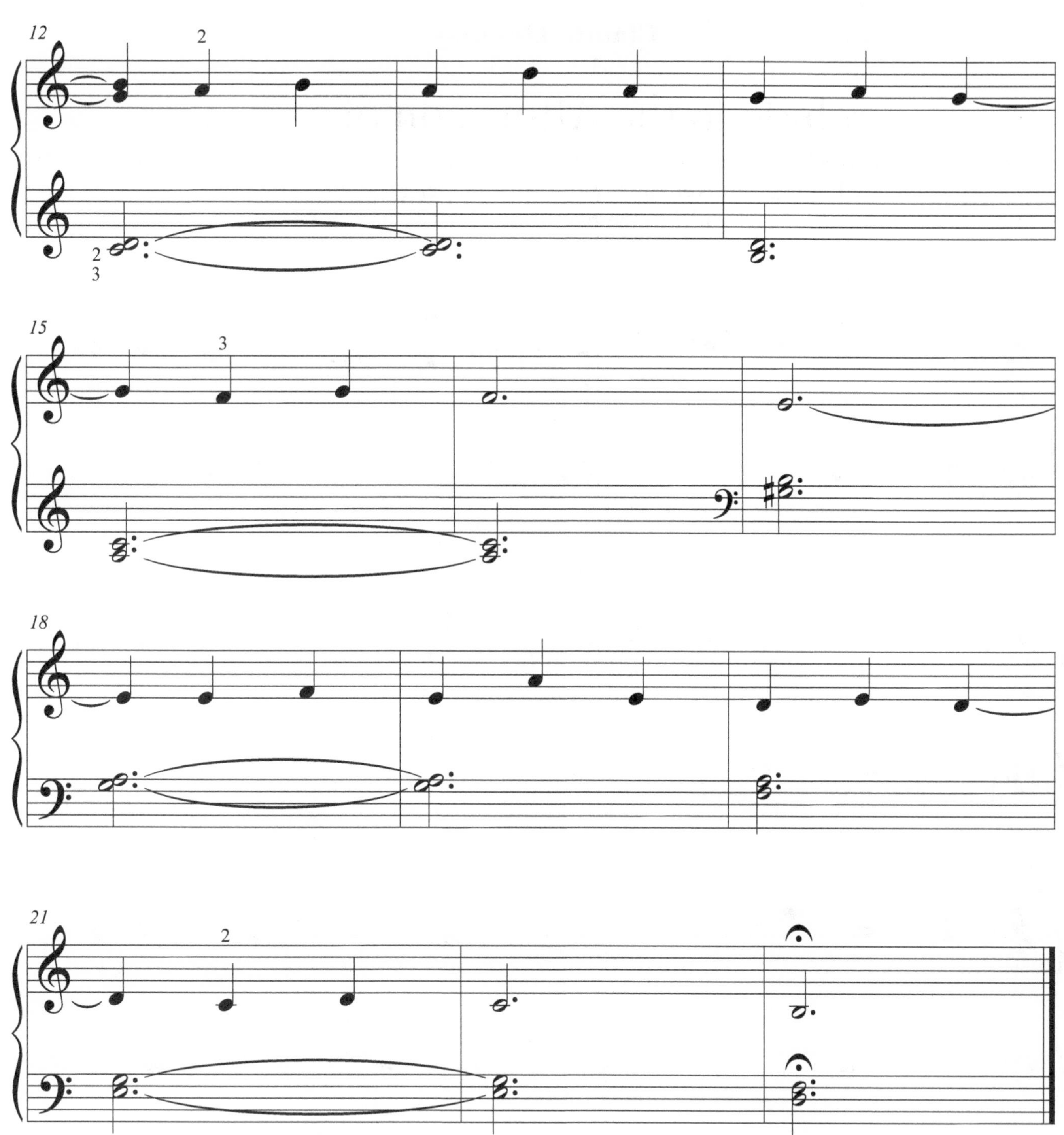
12
2
2
3
15
3
18
21
2

Claude Debussy
1862–1918

Prelude to the Afternoon of a Faun

This chromatically-rich work is a tone-poem based on the Stéphane Mallarmé poem. The story tells of a mythic faun awakening from a hot summer afternoon's nap. Debussy's style is "Impressionistic," a musical parallel to the paintings of artists such as Monet.

Léo Delibes
1836–1891

Flower Duet *from* Lakmé

A popular work, this melody is taken from the opera *Lakmé.* The story is set in India, and this duet is between the main character Lakmé (soprano) and her servant Mallika (mezzo soprano). The sweetness of the music is created by the use of parallel thirds throughout.

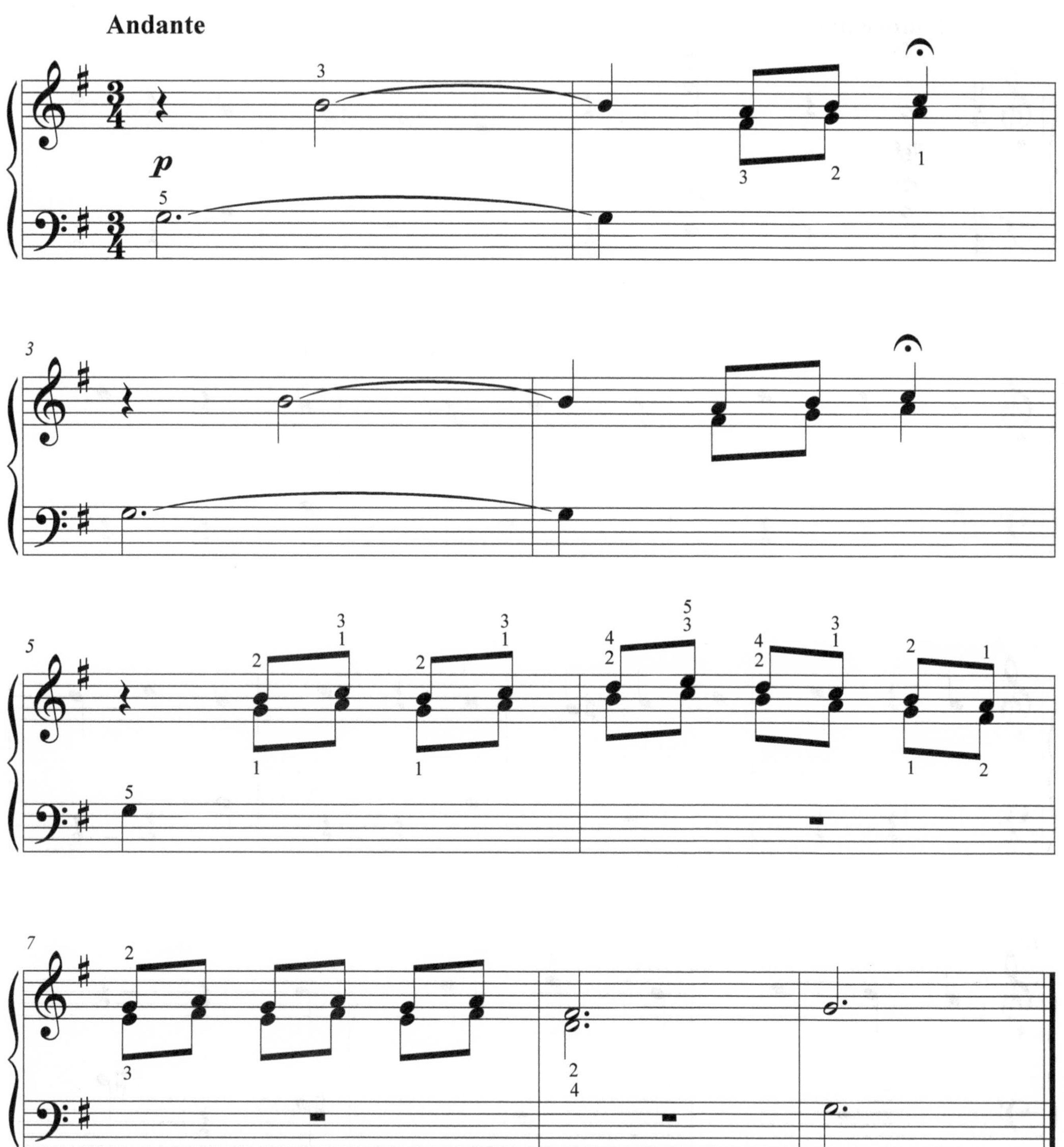

Paul Dukas
1865–1935

Sorcerer's Apprentice

This tone-poem by the French composer Dukas is most-widely known for its depiction in the movie *Fantasia.* The story is based on the poem of the same name written by Johann Wolfgang von Goethe. The melody is played by the bassoon—try to recreate its character.

15
5
5
2
5
2
19
1
22
4
1
2
25
1
3

Antonín Dvořák

1841–1904

Slavonic Dance No. 2

The *Slavonic Dances* are a set of 16 dances originally written for piano four-hands and later orchestrated. In this elegant melody, notice how the notes crest and fall. Add emphasis to the low and high points of each phrase.

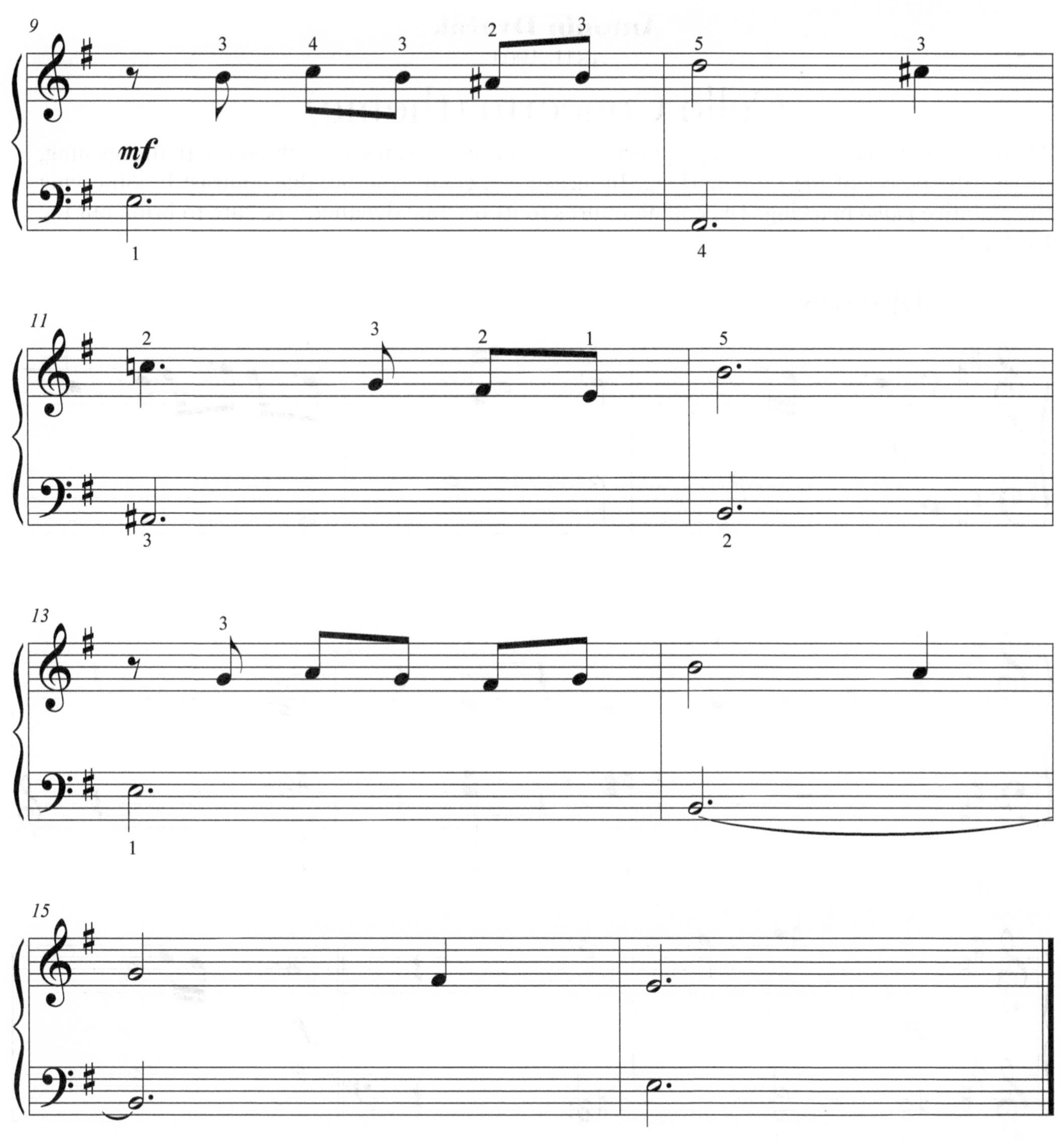
mf

Antonín Dvořák

1841–1904

Cello Concerto (theme)

This majestic concerto offers many opportunities to develop expressive techniques. In the opening, project the power of the *forte* marking. In measure 7, create a noticeable contrast by observing the plaintive *piano* marking. The ending returns to its original dynamic—be sure to bring out the left hand.

Julius Fučík

1872–1916

Entrance of the Gladiators

Originally a military march, this tune has become associated with clowns and circuses over the years. Chromatic notes play a huge role here. The more comfortable you are playing a chromatic scale, the easier this march will be.

Gregorian Chant

Dies Irae

In the late Sixth Century, Pope Gregory I codified the music of the Roman Catholic Church (hence the term "Gregorian.") This melody is taken from the Requiem, served in memory of the departed. The title is Latin for "day of wrath" and has been adapted by many composers, including Berlioz, Mahler, and Rachmaninoff.

Edvard Grieg
1843–1907

In the Hall of the Mountain King

Grieg composed incidental music set to Henrik Ibsen's play *Peer Gynt.* This theme is introduced in the sixth scene of Act II, where the Mountain King confronts the hero Peer. The melody is repeated at the octave, so use the same fingerings as in the beginning.

George Handel
1685–1759

Alleluia Chorus *from* Messiah

The most famous movement of Handel's *Messiah,* it has been bringing audiences to their feet since the London premiere. According to tradition, King George II was so moved by the opening notes of the chorus that he rose to his feet along with the audience. It is still customary for audiences to stand during the performance of this section.

George Handel
1685–1759

Largo *from* Xerxes

Xerxes was commissioned by the King's Theater of London in 1737. The musical innovations used by Handel were thought to be confusing and the work was not received well at the time. After a hiatus of almost 200 years, however, it was revived in 1924.

Joseph Haydn

1732–1809

Allegro *from* Cello Concerto No. 2

Haydn was a major composer of the classical era. Not only was he a close friend of Mozart's, he was also one of Beethoven's teachers. This lovely work reflects his flair for melody.

Joseph Haydn
1732–1809

Gypsy Rondo

This melody is taken from the final movement of Piano Trio No. 39. Like many other composers, Haydn enjoyed the music of Europe's wandering gypsies. The trio ends in a whirlwind of notes, with the melody played faster and faster like a Gypsy dance.

Ruggero Leoncavallo
1857–1919

Aria *from* Pagliacci

Pagliacci is a tragic opera that tells the sad story of a betrayed clown. This aria is entitled *Esti la giubba* ("Put on the costume.") It is sung at the end of the first act when Pagliacci, dressing to go on stage, discovers his betrayal and struggles to still give a performance.

Franz Liszt
1811–1886

Liebestraum

This work is the final of a set of three romantic and lyrical piano pieces. The title is German for "dreams of love." Notice how Liszt creates this mood with a simple melody and just the right number of chromatic notes in the left hand.

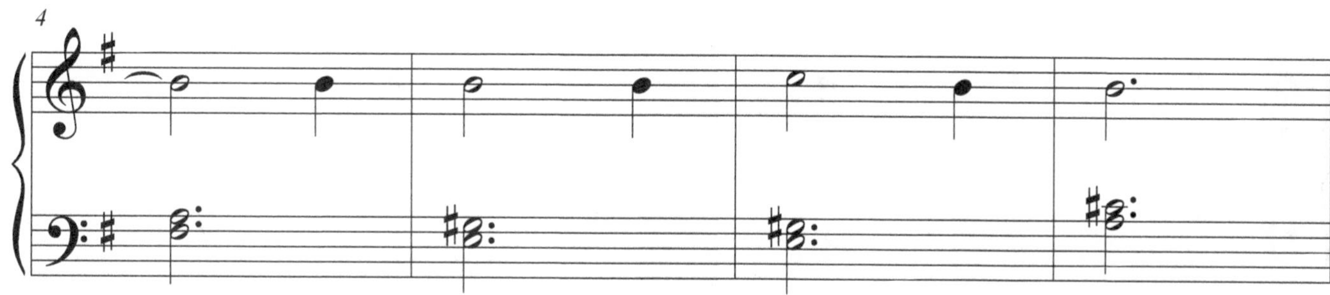

Edward MacDowell
1860–1908

Alla Tarantella

Edward MacDowell is considered one of America's first composers. After studying in France and Germany, he returned to America and was a prominent professor and prolific composer. This charming work is from the collection *12 Piano Works.*

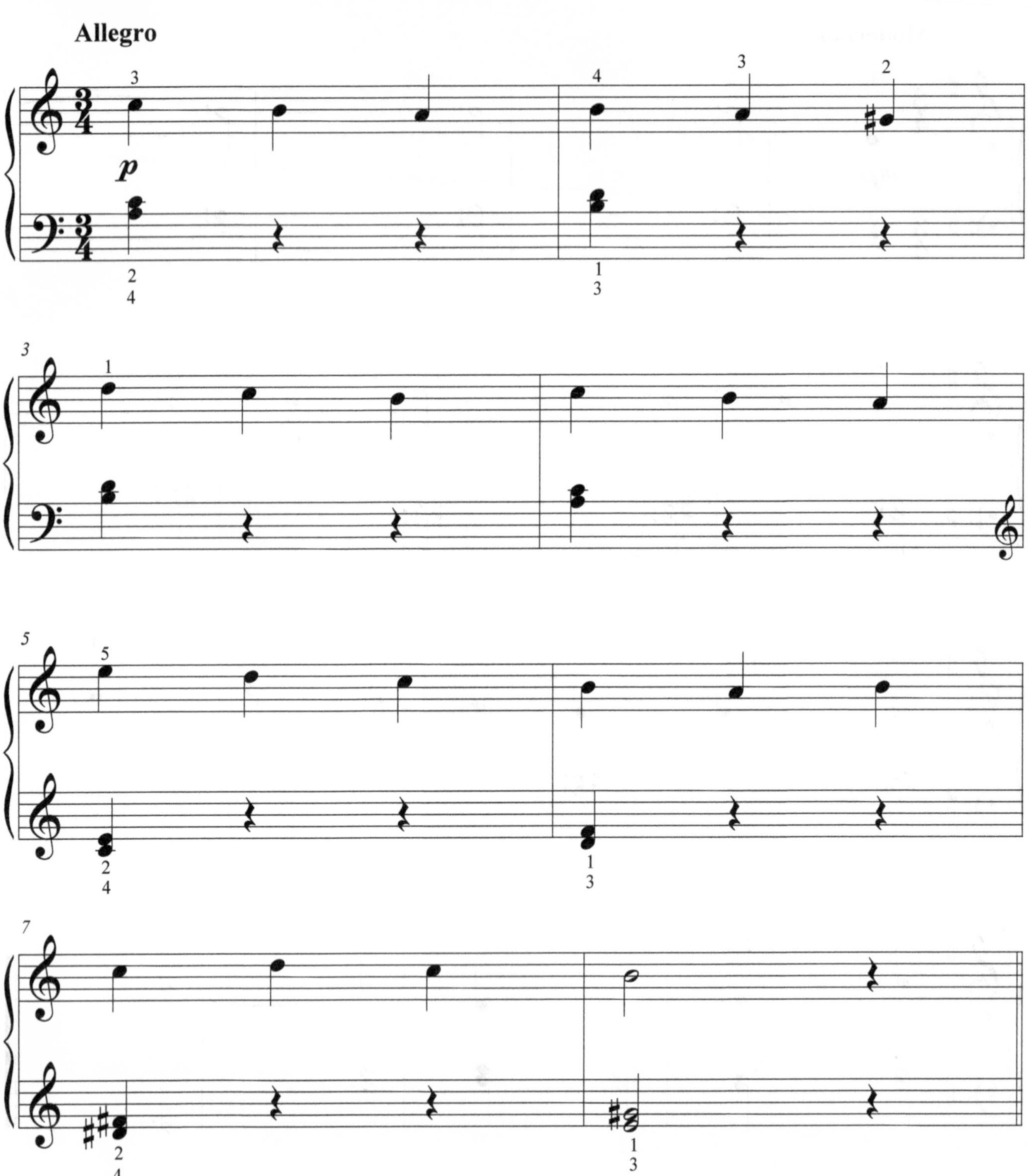

9
mf
p
15
f
18

Felix Mendelssohn
1809–1847

Symphony No. 4 ("Italian")

While on a tour of Italy, Mendelssohn was so inspired by the people and landscapes that he began sketching his fourth symphony, which is also known as the "Italian." The tempo should be upbeat and even. Also, keep the left hand extra light—in the original this part is played *staccato* by the woodwinds.

Felix Mendelssohn
1809–1847

Wedding March

This universally known work has its inspiration in Shakespeare. The *Wedding March* is a movement from a suite of incidental music to the play *A Midsummer Night's Dream.* It became a standard after Princess Victoria, daughter of Queen Victoria, selected it for her wedding in 1858.

Leopold Mozart
1719–1787

Bourrée

Wolfgang Amadeus Mozart's father, Leopold, was an accomplished composer and teacher whose crown student was his son. He wrote many works as educational pieces for young Wolfgang, including this charming *bourrée.* Be mindful of the subtle difference between the *mezzo-forte* and *mezzo-piano* dynamics.

Leopold Mozart
1719–1787

Toy Symphony (theme)

Aside from its playful nature, this symphony earned its nickname for another reason: it was the first ever to incorporate toy instruments! These included a slide whistle, toy trumpet, and even baby rattles. Keep the mood light and graceful, like a music box.

Wolfgang Mozart
1756–1791

Minuet in C

This charming minuet comes from a collection of small pieces named *Nannerl's Notebook*, after the composer's older sister. Amazingly, those small pieces were composed when he was only six years old and were his first works to be published. Hence, they're cataloged as K 1.

mp
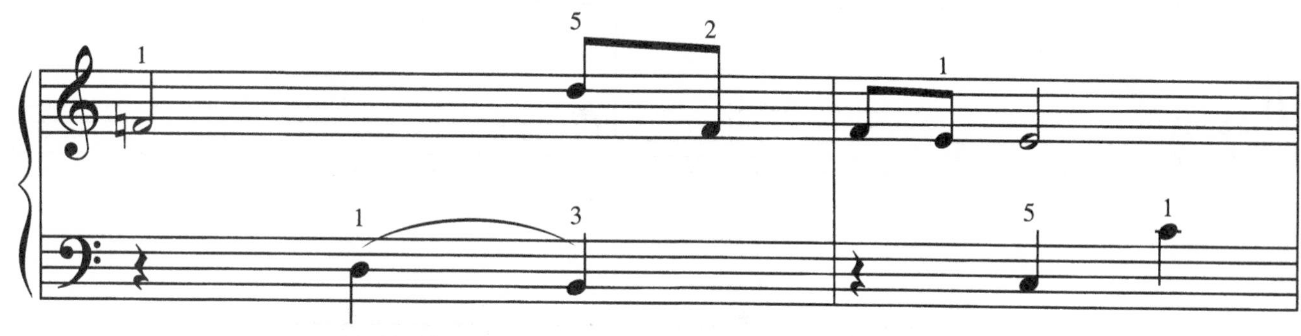

Wolfgang Mozart
1756–1791

Lento *from* Clarinet Concerto

In Mozart's time, the clarinet was a brand new instrument, not widely known. His concerto was the first of its kind and made the clarinet a popular instrument. And remember, a clarinetist has to breathe. Shape your phrases as if you were breathing to the music.

5
4
3
2
1
5
3
2
1

5
4
3
2
1
5
3
2
1

5
4
3
2
1
4
3
5
3
2
1

3
2
4
2
1
2
3
5
1

Wolfgang Mozart
1756–1791

Andante *from* Piano Concerto No. 21

This is one of Mozart's most popular melodies, taken from *Piano Concerto No. 21.* Ever since it was played in a movie it's gained a nickname, "Elvira Madigan". Play it gracefully, and give the two notes with sharps an extra push.

Wolfgang Mozart
1756–1791

Romanze *from* Eine Kleine Nachtmusik

Here is the second movement of *Eine Kleine Nachtmusik*. All together there are four movements. Mozart wrote of a fifth, but it was unfortunately lost. The mood here should be a bit calmer, in contrast to the lively first movement.

Wolfgang Mozart
1756–1791

Glockenspiel *from* The Magic Flute

This piece is from the opera *Magic Flute.* In this scene, Papageno, the feathered bird catcher, appears on stage and plays magical bells that make grumpy people happy again. Play the notes brightly, as if you were playing bells and making grumpy people happy.

Wolfgang Mozart
1756–1791

Symphony No. 25 (opening)

This is the opening to one of Mozart's most famous symphonies. The notes are far apart in the beginning so that the piano can have a nice big sound, almost like a full orchestra. Try to hear the strings playing the crisp syncopation in the beginning.

Wolfgang Mozart
1756–1791

Aria *from* The Marriage of Figaro

Here is an aria from *Marriage of Figaro* where one of the characters compares his love to a butterfly and promises to "never let her fly away again". Listen to how Mozart paints the image of a butterfly flying and landing by having the melody rise up and then flutter back down.

Modest Mussorgsky
1839–1881

Boris Godunov (opening)

Boris Godunow is an opera rich in Russian musical traditions: lyrical melodies, minor keys, and extra-deep roles sung by *basso profundos.* The story tells of political upheaval and intrigue in Medieval Russia. When playing the left hand, try to hear a bassoon as in the original.

Modest Mussorgsky
1839–1881

Promenade *from* Pictures at an Exhibition

Moussorgsky composed a suite of piano pieces inspired by a show of the complete works of artist Viktor Hartmann. This melody is played in the opening, and in between movements musically depicting a stroll from one painting to another. The entire suite was later orchestrated by Maurice Ravel. The orchestrated version is the most widely known.

Michał Oginsky

1765–1833

Polonaise

This elegant and sophisticated-sounding *polonaise* was written by a Polish statesmen and diplomat who was also an avid music lover and composer. Before playing, notice the accidentals and plan your fingering accordingly. Also, warm-up with an E minor arpeggio before practicing this piece.

Giovanni Pescetti

1704–1766

Sonata

Giovanni Pescetti was an 18th century organist and composer who lived in Venice and then London. Amongst his students was the famous Antonio Salieri. This excerpt is the opening of the third movement of the Sonata in C Minor.

Amilcare Ponchielli
1834–1886

Dance of the Hours

A staple of the repertoire, this dance appears in Act III, Scene II of Ponchielli's ballet *La Gioconda.* However, most people will recognize its parody by Allan Sherman. In this scene, guests are being received in a large and luxurious ballroom.

Sergei Rachmaninoff
1873–1943

Vocalise

This mesmerizing work is the last in a set of fourteen songs. In the original, there are no words for the singer to sing; rather, Rachmaninoff specified that any vowel of the performer's choosing would suffice. Keep the tempo even, and be extra lyrical with the melody.

Nikolai Rimsky-Korsakov

1844–1908

Russian Easter Overture (theme)

Rimsky-Korsakov wrote an orchestral fantasy on Easter themes entitled *Russian Easter Overture.* The Russian hymn heard in the theme, "Let God Arise," is one of several used. Note the contrast between the solo voice in the opening, and the chorale beginning at measure 8.

Reverently

Nikolai Rimsky-Korsakov

1844–1908

Scheherazade

This popular Rimsky-Korsakov work is based on *The Book of One Thousand and One Nights.* In the story, a doomed Sultan's wife postpones her end by telling the sultan a story so intriguing it lasted 1,001 evenings. Be mindful of how the notes with sharps color the melody.

Moderato

mp

Gioachino Rossini

1792–1868

William Tell Overture

Rossini's opera is based on the legend of William Tell, the Swiss crossbow marksmen famed for being able to split apples off of people's heads with an arrow. The first section is the opening of the opera, painting a calm and serene country scene. The second and third are part of the "cavalry" movement, and should be played with a gallop.

I. Calmly

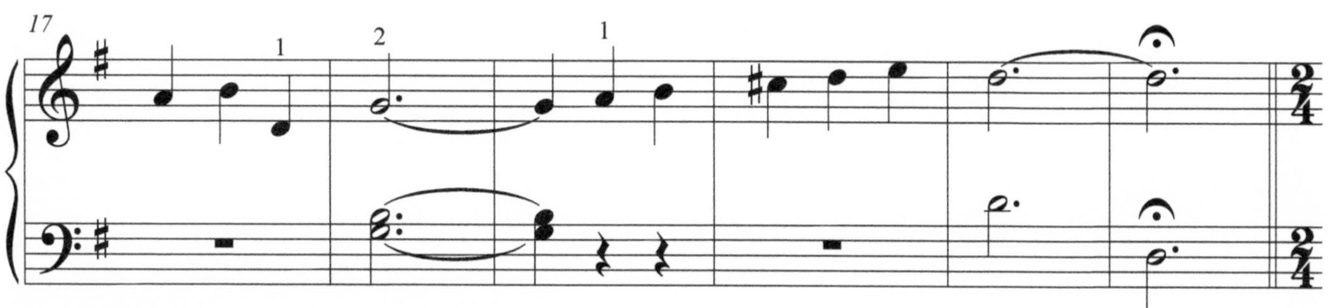

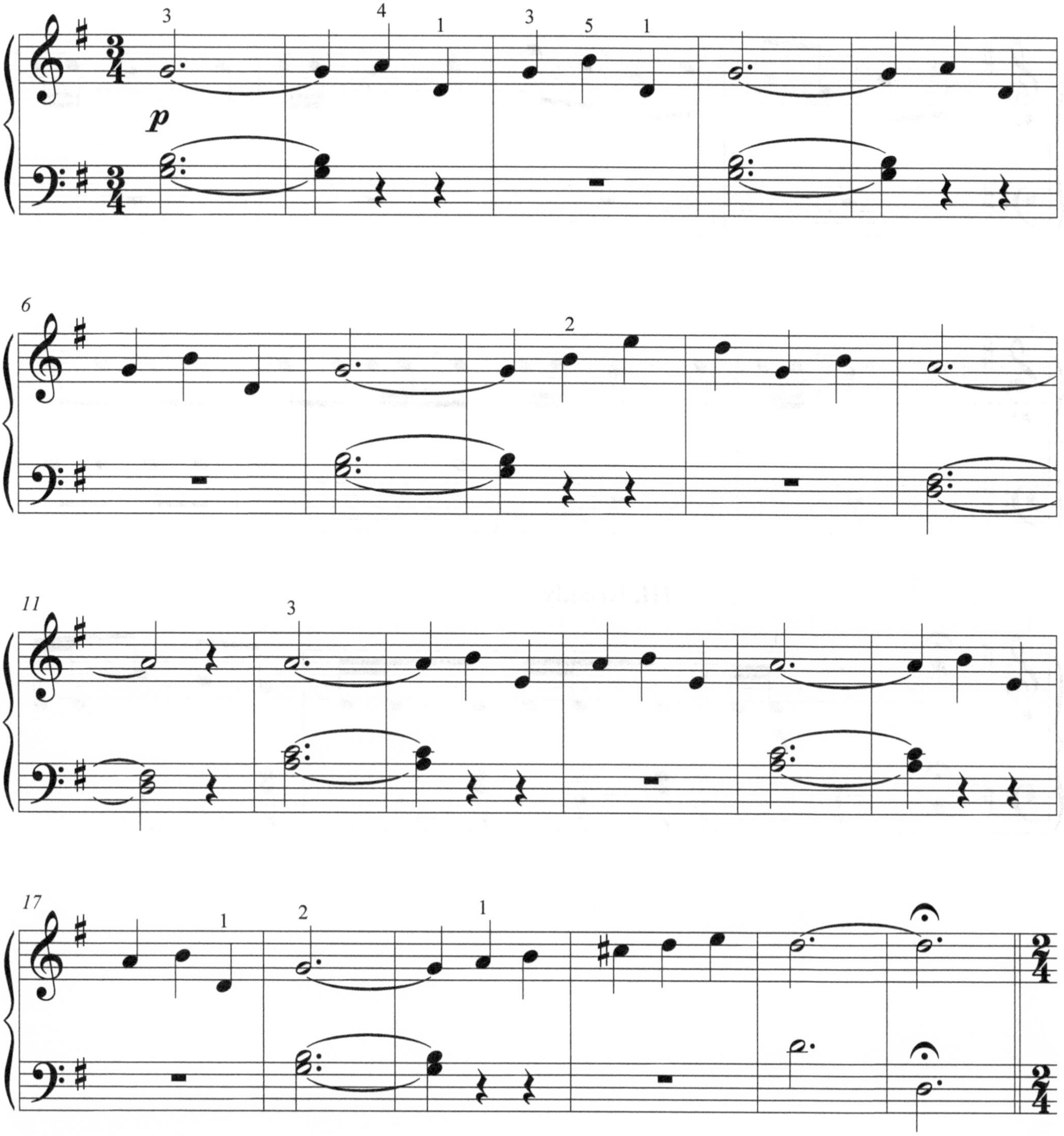

II. Allegro

III. Briskly

38
42
45
49

Camille Saint-Saëns
1835–1921

Danse Macabre

A dark work, this piece is part of a tone-poem inspired by the works of poet Henri Cazalis. In the orchestral version, the violin represents death making his annual visit during Halloween. This melody is played by a solo violinist, calling the rest of the orchestra to the dance.

Camille Saint-Saëns

1835–1921

Elephant *from* Carnival of the Animals

"Elephant" is the fifth movement of the suite *Carnival of the Animals.* Saint-Saëns composed 30 short pieces, depicting animals such as swans, tortoises, and kangaroos. It's quite easy to see the musical picture of an elephant that has been written.

Andante

Erik Satie
1866–1925

Gymnopédie No. 1

This is the first in a series of three works, with the title hinting at Greek antiquity. Each is an ambient piece, creating a mood rather than telling a story. Play the right hand lightly, and keep the sway of the left hand steady.

Domenico Scarlatti
1685–1757

Sonata in C Major ("The Hunt")

The open harmonies (4ths, 5ths, and 6ths) throughout this work are meant to mimic hunting horns. Keep the tempo brisk, and contrast the ***mp*** middle section with the ***f*** of the others. Also, consider the possibility of playing two notes on one hand to ease performance.

Franz Schubert

1797–1828

The Erlking

Schubert set this poem by Goethe to music, and is believed to be his first published composition. In the poem, an ill boy is being carried on horseback and begins to see visions as his condition worsens. The repetition in the right hand is known as an ostinato and conveys the sense of a speeding horse.

9
11
13
2
15
1

Franz Schubert
1797–1828

The Doppelganger

This work is part of the *Schwanengesang,* a posthumous collection of Schubert's songs. *Der Doppelganger* is the title of a Heinrich Heine poem, and means "double" or "look-alike." Play as if you were singing, with your piano phrasing matching your breathing.

Franz Schubert
1797–1828

Symphony No. 8 ("Unfinished")

Schubert's Symphony No. 8 is nicknamed "Unfinished" because it contains only two movements, rather than the traditional four. Although sketches of other movements have been discovered, the work was put aside and never completed. However, Schubert did complete a ninth symphony.

Robert Schumann
1810–1856

Child Falling Asleep *from* Scenes from Childhood

With so many children, Clara and Robert Schumann had much practice putting them to bed. Schumann creates a lulling effect with a repeated passage in the right hand known as an *ostinato*. This piece ends on a peaceful, eye-shutting major chord.

Slowly and Gently

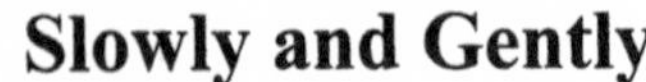

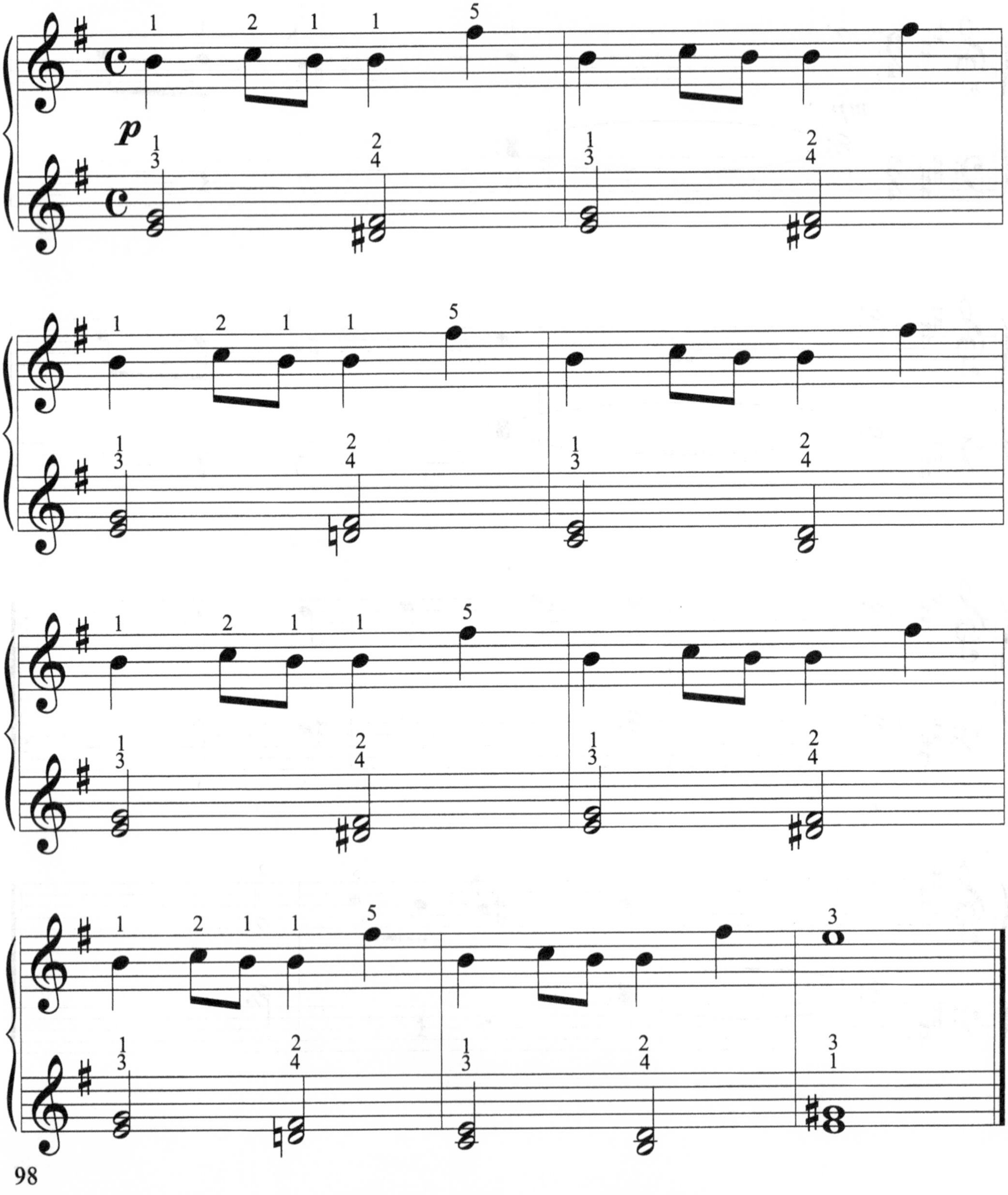

Robert Schumann

1810–1856

Piano Concerto (opening)

Schumann was a very promising young pianist. Unfortunately, he permanently injured his right hand and couldn't perform. Although he wrote many short piano pieces, he wrote only one concerto.

Robert Schumann
1810–1856

Der Arme Peter

The title of this piece means "Poor Peter" and is the setting of a Heinrich Heine poem. It tells the sad story of a boy walking through a village, disappointed over his lost love. Keep the mood pastoral and melancholic.

mf

Robert Schumann
1810–1856

Horseman *from* Album for the Young

Dynamics are always key to musical interpretation. This work recreates the sound of a passing horseman by getting louder during the approach and softer for the departure. The heavy and light sections emphasize this image.

Short and brisk

ff
R.H. 1
sim.
mf
mp
p
pp

Robert Schumann

1810–1856

Eusubius *from* Carnaval

This may be the first time you've seen a $\frac{7}{4}$ time signature, but don't be nervous. It's simply a melody that is three beats plus four. Follow the dashed lines when counting and you'll be able to subdivide the measures easily.

Bendřich Smetana

1824–1884

The Moldau

Bedřich Smetana was a Czech composer who strove to portray his homeland in a nationalistic style of romanticism. This melody is the second in a series of tone poems called *Má Vlast* ("My Homeland.") The Moldau is a river in Smetana's native Bohemia, and is represented by the twists and turns of the melody.

Johann Strauss

1825–1899

Blue Danube Waltz

Johan Strauss was a prolific composer of light music, with over 500 published works. His music was so popular in Vienna, that during his lifetime he was named the "Waltz King." Amazingly, one of the world's favorite waltzes was only tepidly received at its premiere.

Moderato

mf

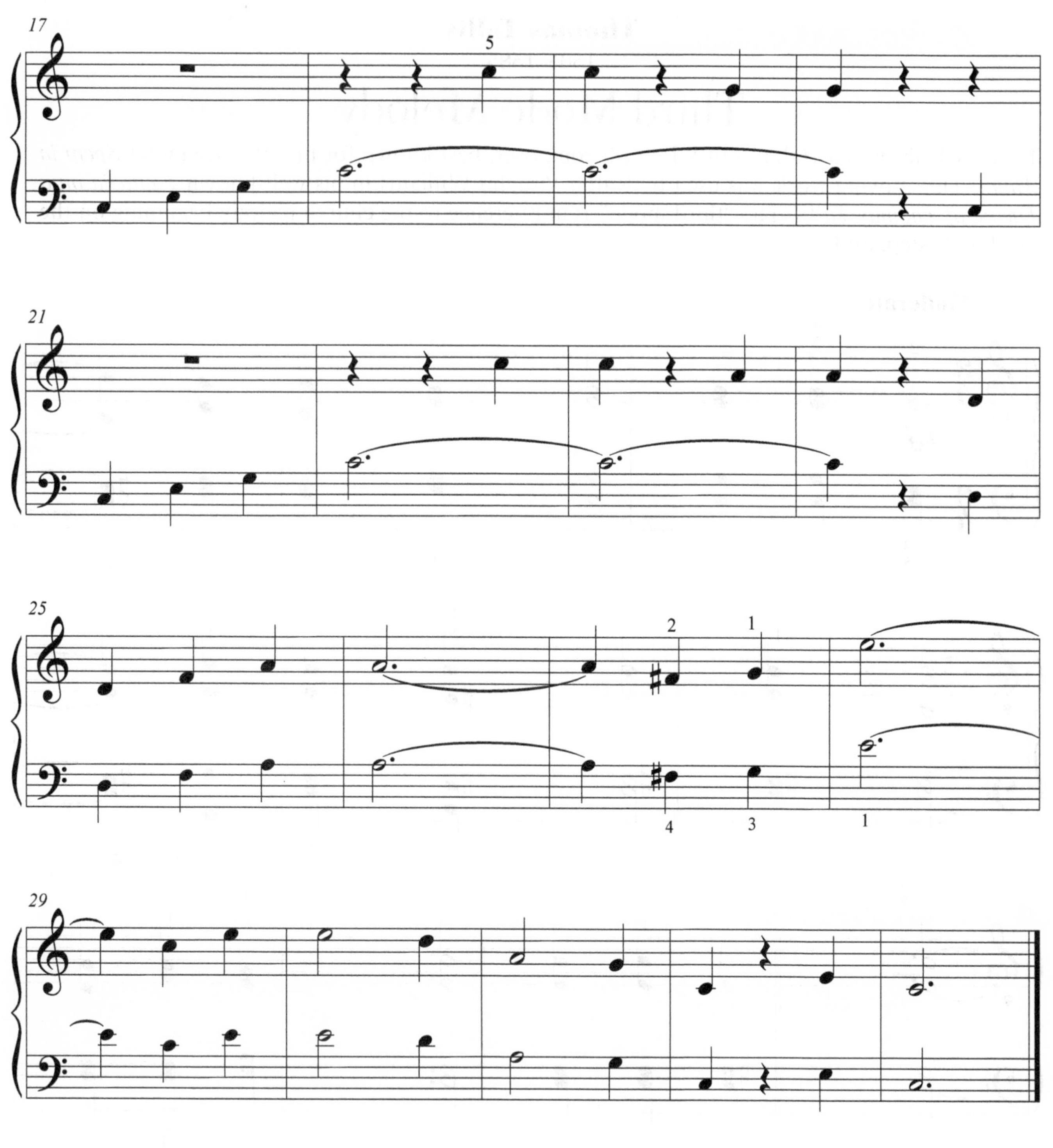
17
21
25
29

Thomas Tallis
1505–1585

Third Mode Melody

Thomas Tallis was a 16th Century English composer, best known for his 40-voice motet *Spem in Alium.* This moving work was used by Ralph Vaughn Williams in his well-known *Fantasia on a Theme of Thomas Tallis.* The "third mode" is in reference to the church melody beginning on the third scale step, an E.

Pyotr Tchaikovsky
1840–1893

Piano Concerto (theme)

Tchaikovsky finished his first piano concerto in February, 1875. The famous melody is based on a peasant melody the composer heard at a market near Kiev. Use the *ritardando (rit.)* at the end to softly bring the melody to an end.

Pyotr Tchaikovsky
1840–1893

Piano Concerto, Mvt. II (theme)

The second movement of the piano concerto is a gentle melody used to contrast the energy of the previous movement. The *molto ritardando* calls for a great reduction in tempo, and the *a tempo* brings it back to the original pulse. Fast and slow can be used to contrast sections just as effectively as loud and soft.

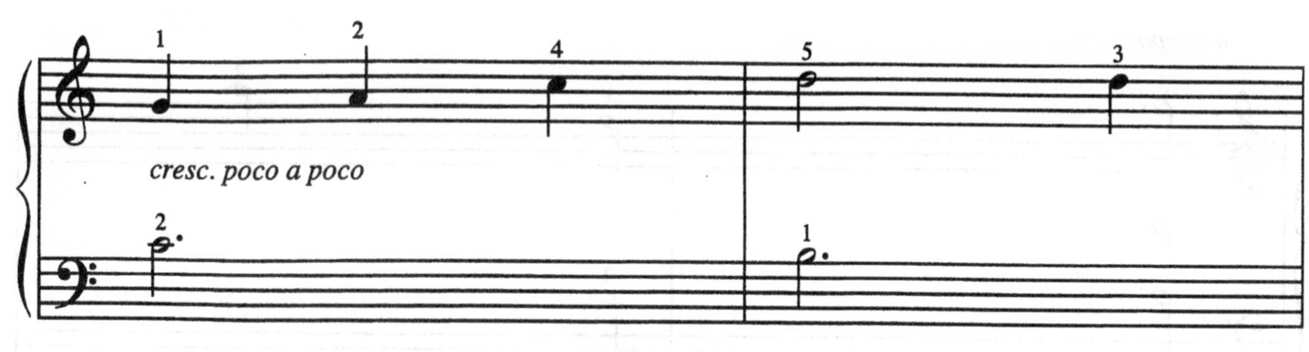

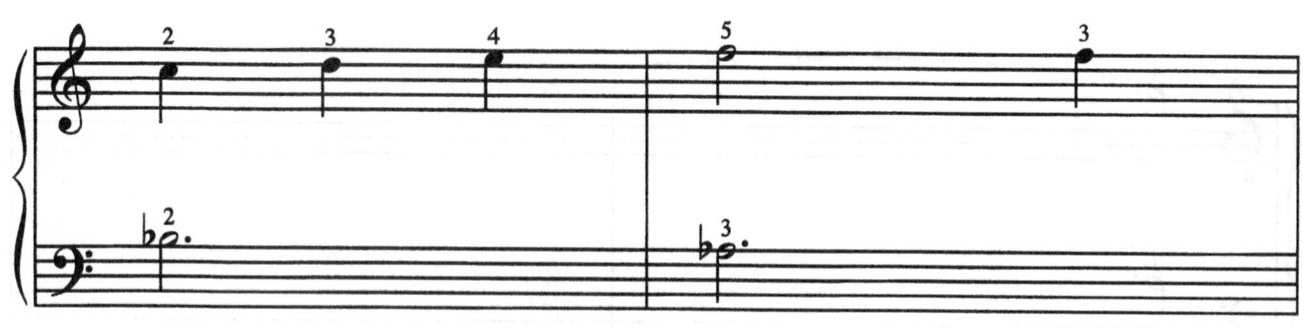

molto rit.

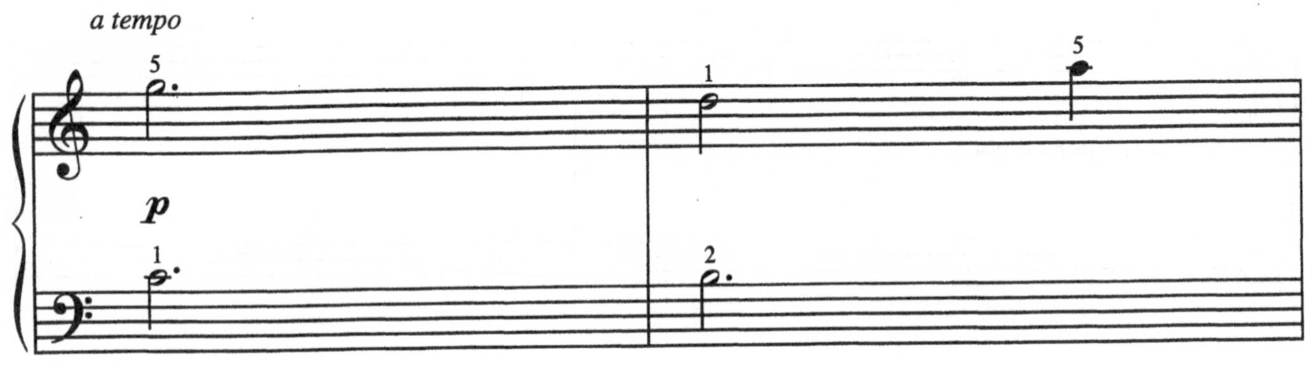
a tempo
5
1
5
p
1
2

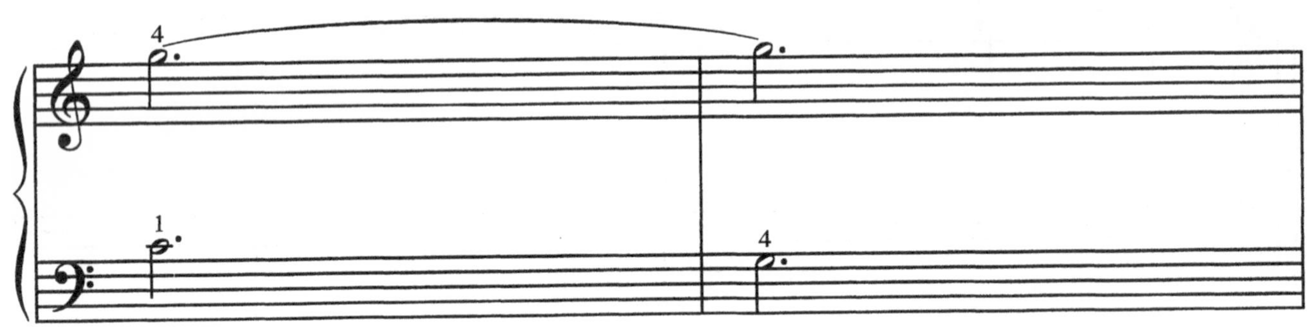
4
1
4

3
2
1
5
5
1
2

1
1
4

1
2
4
5
3
1
2

2
3
4
5
1
3

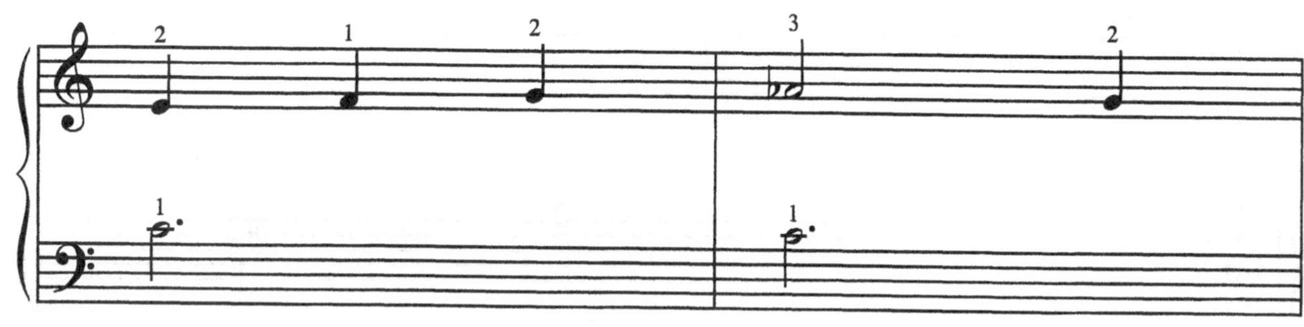
2
1
2
3
2
1
1

2
2
1

Pyotr Tchaikovsky
1840–1893

Sleeping Beauty Waltz

This beautiful waltz is from Tchaikovsky's famous ballet *Sleeping Beauty*. You've no doubt heard it before on many different occasions. Keep the tempo steady, and be expressive as you sharply slow the tempo at the *rallantando (rall.)*.

Moderato

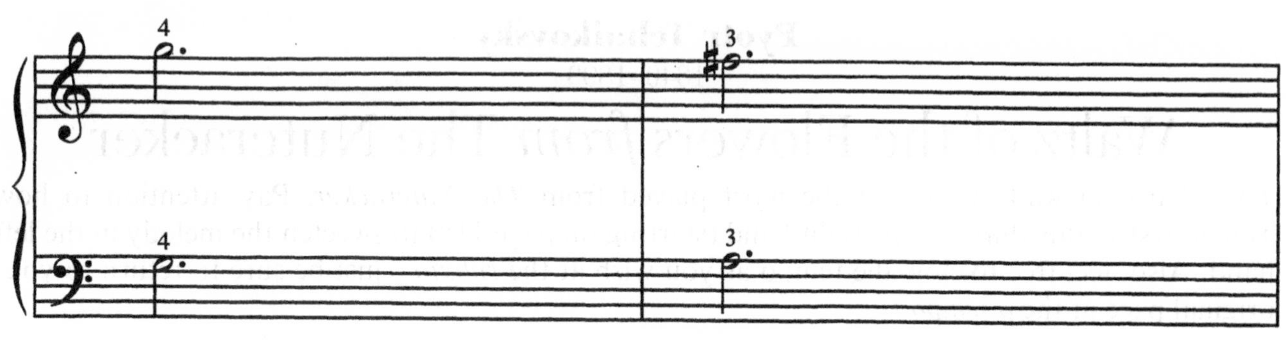
4
3
4
3

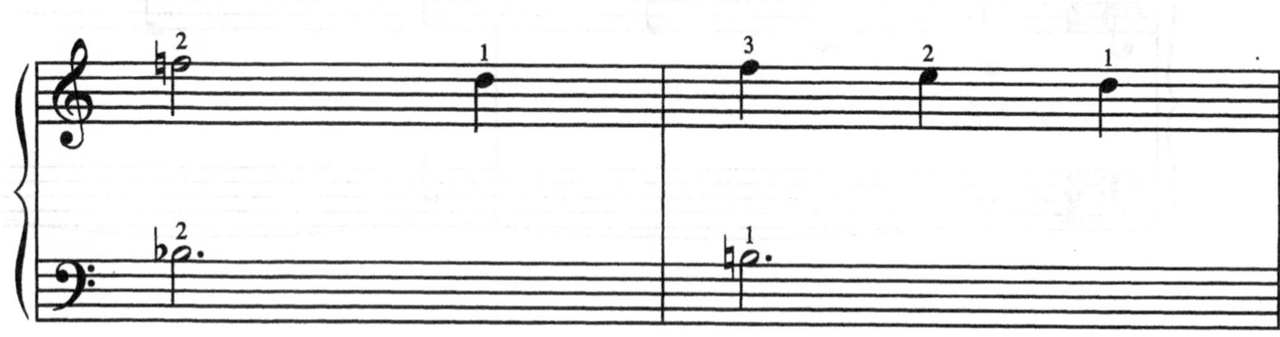
2
1
3
2
1
2
1

5
4
3
2
4
3

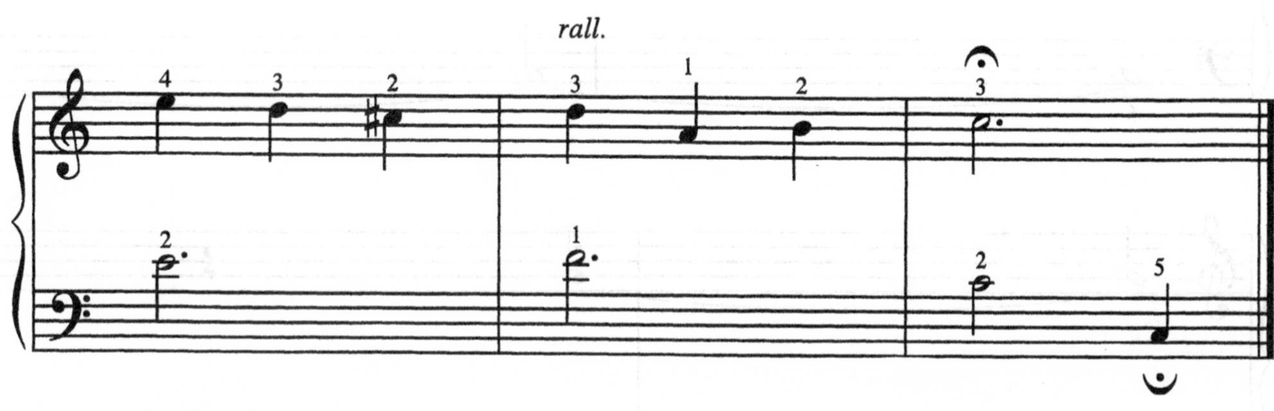
rall.
4
3
2
3
1
2
3
2
1
2
5

Pyotr Tchaikovsky
1840–1893

Waltz of the Flowers *from* The Nutcracker

This charming waltz is one of the most played from *The Nutcracker.* Pay attention to how Tchaikovsky adds thirds in the right hand (starting on page 118) to sweeten the melody in the left hand. Also, feel free to slow the tempo as you wish at the *rubato*—just be sure to return to your original pace at the *a tempo.*

mp
mf
rubato
f

a tempo
mp

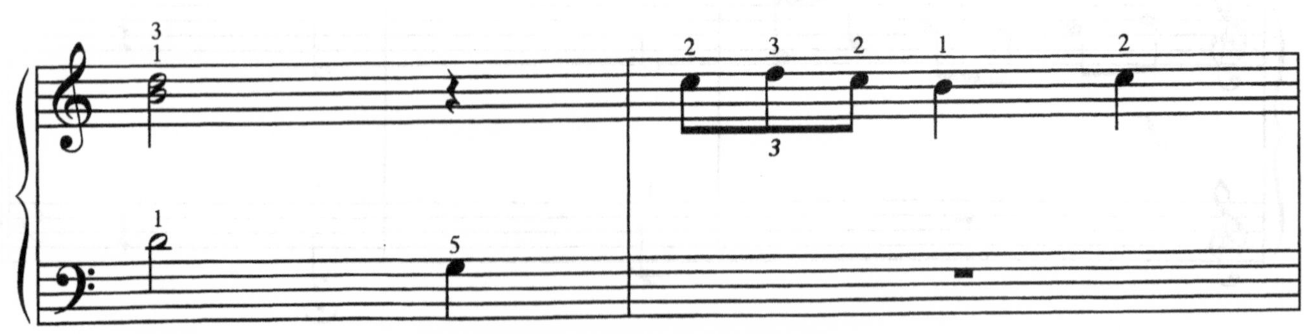

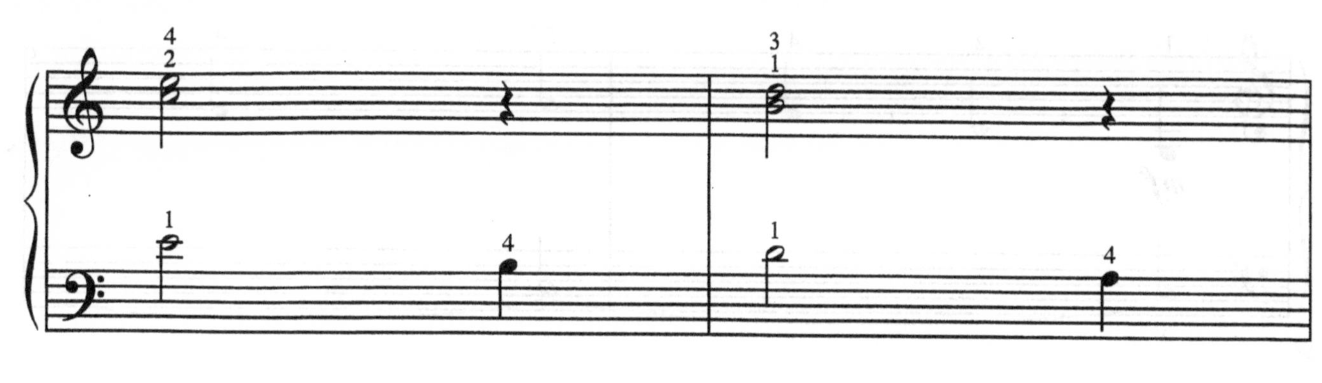

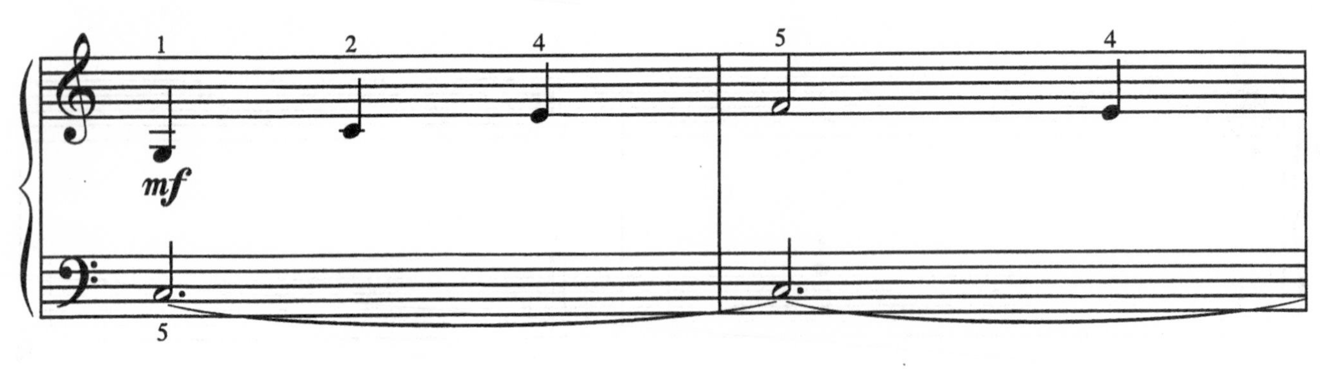
1
2
4
5
4
mf
5

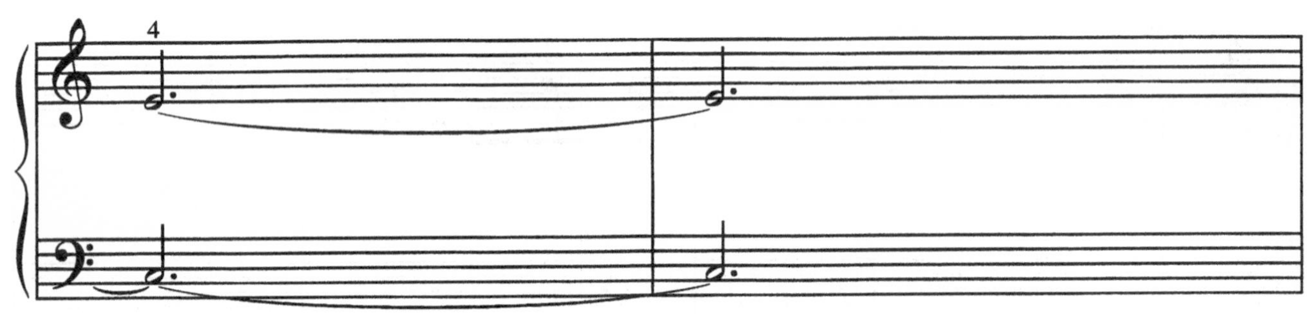
4

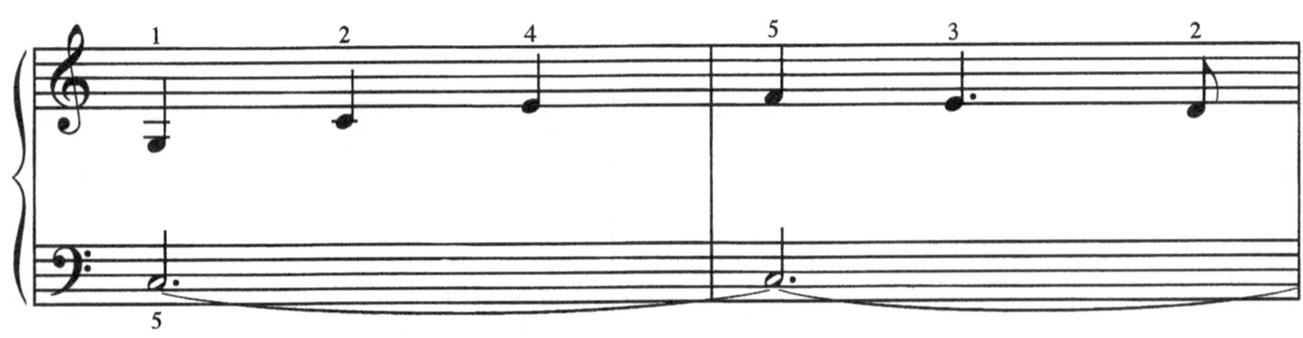
1
2
4
5
3
2
5

5

mp
mf
f

Giuseppe Verdi

1813–1901

Aria *from* Rigoletto

This popular aria is from Verdi's *Rigoletto,* which premiered in 1851 and helped solidify the composer's fame. *La Donna é Mobile* means "woman is fickle," with the inherent irony being that the Duke singing it is himself the ficklest character of the story. Many famous tenors, from Enrico Carruso to Luciano Pavarotti, have recorded this work.

Antonio Vivaldi

1678–1741

Spring *from* The Four Seasons

The *Four Seasons* is a set of four works for solo violin and string orchestra depicting each of the seasons. This is the melody from the first movement, "Spring." No doubt familiar, keep the tempo upbeat and use dynamics to contrast the varying sections.

9
11
f
13
16

Richard Wagner
1813–1883

March *from* Tannhäuser

Tannhäuser is an opera based on a mythical *meistersinger* of the same name who stumbled upon Venus' secret mountain-lair on Earth. Mythology played a huge role in Wagner's operas, creating a host of characters similar to today's comic books. The introduction here is played by trumpets and should be kept military-like.

Slightly slower
mf

Richard Wagner

1813–1883

Ride of the Valkyries

One of Wagner's most popular melodies, this majestic work is from *The Valkyrie,* which is the second of the four "Ring Cycle" operas. Valkyries were mythological Norse female warrior-gods, integral in the four operas of the story. The melody essentially outlines an arpeggio, and should soar to its climax.

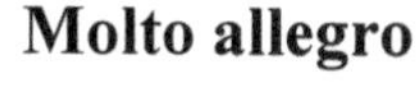

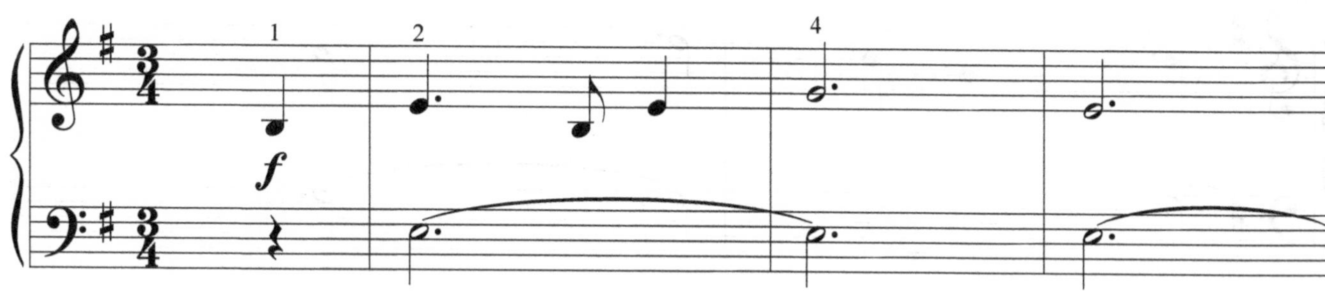

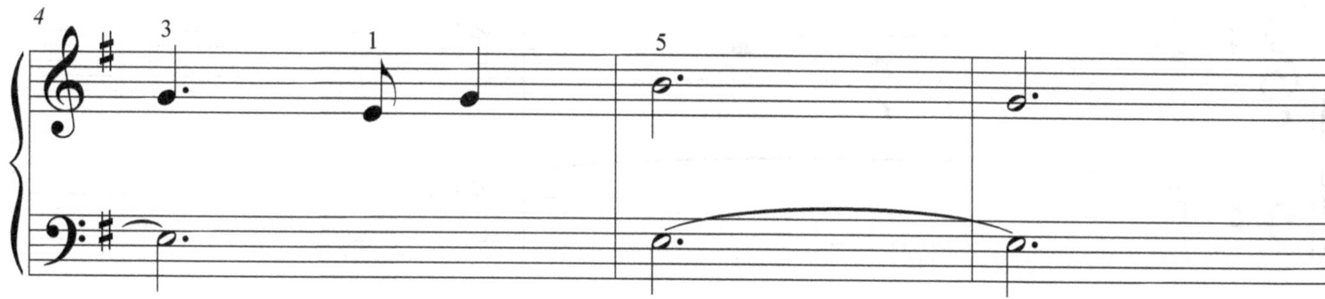

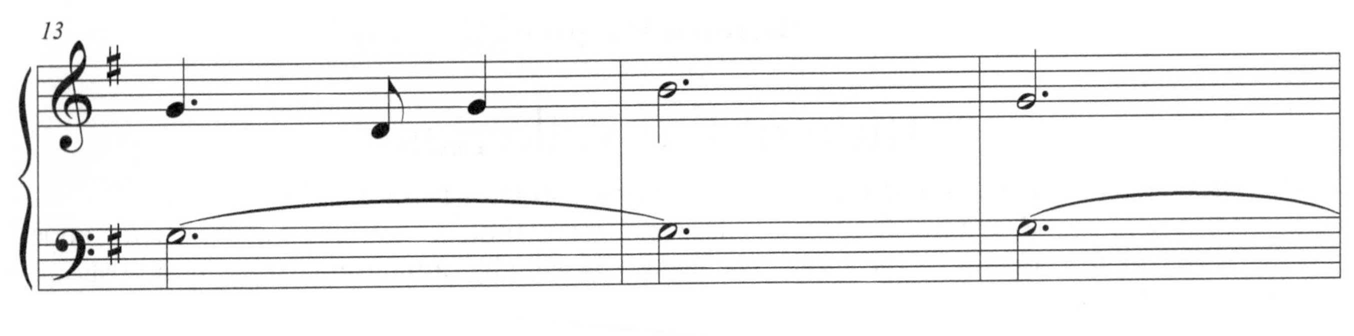
13

16

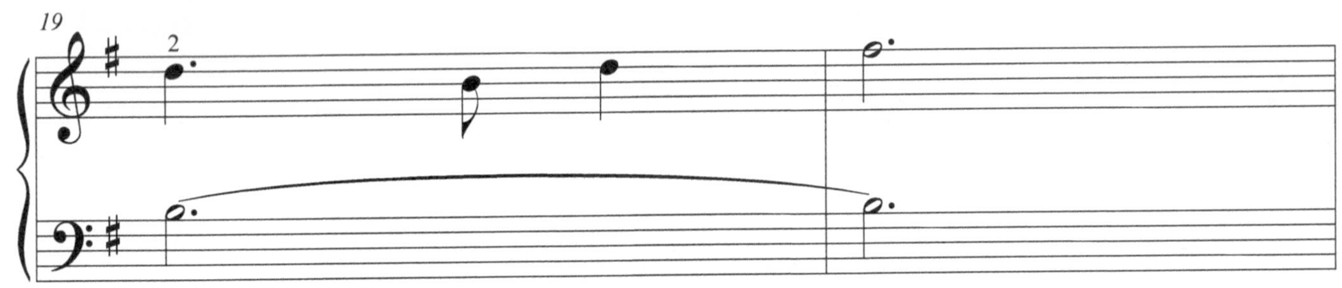
19
2

21

NOTES

NOTES

NOTES

NOTES

NOTES

NOTES